P9-BZR-642

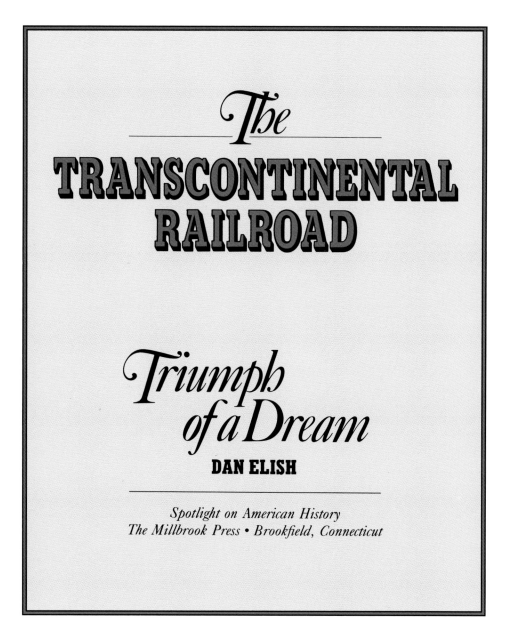

The
TRANSCONTINENTAL RAILROAD

Triumph of a Dream

DAN ELISH

Spotlight on American History
The Millbrook Press • Brookfield, Connecticut

Published by The Millbrook Press
2 Old New Milford Road, Brookfield, Connecticut 06804

Cover photo courtesy of The Granger Collection
Photos courtesy of The Oakland Museum: pp. 6, 9, 41, 44, 48,
51; Bridgeman Art Library/Art Resource, NY: p. 12; The Granger
Collection: pp. 14, 16, 57; de Grummond Children's Literature
Research Collection of the McCain Library/Archives, University
of Southern Mississippi: p. 20; Southern Pacific Transportation
Company: pp. 21, 33; Library of Congress: pp. 28, 53, 54 (right);
Bettmann Archive: p. 34; "Snow Sheds on the Central Pacific Railroad
in the Sierra Nevada Mountains" by Joseph Becker, Thomas Gilcrease
Museum, Tulsa, Oklahoma: p. 38; St. Louis Mercantile Library
Association: p. 43; Union Pacific Museum: p. 54 (left).

Map courtesy of Joe LeMonnier

Library of Congress Cataloging-in-Publication Data
Elish, Dan.
The transcontinental railroad : triumph of a dream / Dan Elish.
p.   cm.— (Spotlight on American history)
Includes bibliographical references and index.
Summary: Describes the efforts to build the first railroad to link
the eastern and western United States and the obstacles that had
to be overcome in the process.
ISBN 1-56294-337-5 (lib. bdg.)
1. Pacific railroads—Juvenile literature. [1. Pacific
railroads. 2. Railroads—History.] I. Title. II. Series.
TF25.P23E38 1993 385'.0973—dc20 92-39995 CIP AC

Contents

The
TRANSCONTINENTAL RAILROAD

The Central Pacific's Jupiter *(foreground) and the Union Pacific's* No. 119 *sit motionless on the tracks as the ceremony begins.*

1

THE GOLDEN SPIKE

The one-street town of Promontory, Utah, was buzzing with activity on May 10, 1869. A crowd of one thousand people lined the streets. Reporters from nearly every paper in the country were on hand. A band from Salt Lake City raised its trombones and trumpets, ready to play. Top-level railroad executives milled about, waiting for the ceremony to begin—the ceremony that would mark the completion of the transcontinental railroad.

Work on this great project had begun a full eight years before. The Central Pacific line had started in San Francisco and built east, while the Union Pacific Railroad had started in Omaha, Nebraska, and built west. Now these two great lines were to finally meet and for the first time in history connect the eastern and western United States.

And now, the crowd—mostly Irish and Chinese laborers who had borne the brunt of the work—pushed close.

"Gentlemen," said Leland Stanford, president of the Central Pacific, "with your assistance we will proceed to lay the last tie, the last rail, and drive the last spike."

With great pomp, Stanford picked up a silver-headed sledgehammer, lifted it over his head, aimed at a gold spike, and swung with all his might . . . only to miss!

The Irish and Chinese workers howled. Stanford was getting a taste of just how hard it was to build a railroad.

Now Thomas Durant, the vice president of the Union Pacific, took up the sledgehammer, and swung a mighty blow.

He missed as well.

As a worker was hastily summoned to pound in the final spike, a telegrapher sent the signal to the nation: "It's done!"

From New York to San Francisco the country cheered as one.

Back at Promontory, two great locomotives inched forward just close enough so that the two engineers could lean forward and shake hands with each other.

A San Francisco author, Bret Harte, wrote a poem to commemorate the event:

> *What was it the engines said,*
> *Pilots touching, head to head,*
> *Facing on a single track,*
> *Half a world behind each back?*

It was the joining of two worlds: East meets West. Before the railroad, Americans thought of the West as a wilderness populated mostly by Indians. On that day the fabric of American life changed forever. Farmers and ranchers had a new, more efficient way to send their goods to market. Settlers rushed west, and western cities grew up. America finally had the technological means to grow and thrive—and become the America that we know today. For the first time in history, a vast country was made one.

Chief engineers Grenville Dodge (right) and Samuel S. Montague
in a symbolic handshake joining East and West.

Celebrations lasted for days. Chicago sported a 7-mile (11-kilometer) parade. New York ordered a hundred-gun salute in City Hall Park, and business was suspended on Wall Street for the day. The residents of Buffalo ran through the streets singing "The Star Spangled Banner."

It was an astounding event, considering that those who first suggested the idea of a transcontinental railroad were written off as mad dreamers. After all, how could a railroad possibly be built across the country? Who would pay for it? Who would do the work? How would the rails cross over the Rocky Mountains?

Such skepticism was understandable. After all, railroads were still a relatively new phenomenon. To fully understand the immensity of the transcontinental achievement and to grasp the tremendous impact it had on the nation, it is necessary to investigate the beginnings of steam power in America.

2

THE IRON HORSE

Although the Pilgrims landed at Plymouth Rock in 1620, it took a good hundred years before there were roads through the towering forests and mountain passes of North America. As late as 1756, it still took three days to make the 90-mile (145-kilometer) trip between New York and Philadelphia.

Roads gradually improved, but travel by ship was faster and cheaper. Big news was made when the Erie Canal opened for business in 1825. Known as the "Big Ditch," this man-made waterway stretched from Albany on the Hudson River to Buffalo on Lake Erie. Canal boats could make the trip in five days, as opposed to the twenty it took wagons.

The Erie Canal was a triumph of engineering, constructed over eight years at great sacrifice. But Americans wanted something even better—a way to transport goods quickly over land. But how?

Little did they know that a British inventor, Richard Trevithick, had already started down the road to an answer: steam power. In 1804, Trevithick hooked a steam locomotive to a load of iron and pulled his freight 9 miles (14 kilometers) at 5 miles (8 kilometers) per hour.

An artist's interpretation of Richard Trevithick's
1809 circular railway known as "Catch me who can."

This was the beginning of the age of the railroad, the era of the iron horse.

But America was slow to pick up on English success. In the late 1820s, with "canal fever" sweeping the country, nobody was thinking much about railroads.

Only the Delaware & Hudson Canal Company was interested in this new method of transport. In the mid-1820s they sent one of their best young engineers, Horatio Allen, to England to investigate. Allen returned to the states a few years later with four locomotive engines and then, in 1829, to the sound of great cheers, drove one of them at a speed of 10 miles (16 kilometers) an hour over a poorly built, shaky bridge.

That was all other American companies needed to see. Almost overnight, railroad workers were hired to survey possible routes, and very quickly steam power came to dominate the Northeast.

As railroads multiplied, striking innovations were made. Matthais Baldwin, a New Jersey manufacturer, built the first locomotive that could go 60 miles (96 kilometers) an hour, an unheard-of speed in those days.

What of night travel? Until the invention of the headlight, locomotives pushed a flatcar ahead of them with a fire on it to light the way.

And that shrill whistle we all associate with the locomotive? The "voice" of the iron horse was discovered accidentally by an engineer fiddling with a steam valve. By releasing a certain amount of pressure, the famous whistle would pierce the air and announce the train's arrival.

And then there were the tracks. At first, there was no agreement as to how wide the rails should be. The Charleston line laid theirs 5 feet (1.5 meters) apart, the Camden line 4 feet 10 inches (1.47 meters), while the New York & Erie settled on 6 feet (1.8 meters). It was impossible to transfer cars from one line to another! It took a full forty years before all American rail lines were standardized at 4 feet 8½ inches (1.43 meters).

TOM THUMB

IT WAS PETER COOPER, a New Yorker, who in the late 1820s was responsible for a major locomotive breakthrough. Cooper invented a steam engine small enough to negotiate sharp curves earlier locomotives couldn't manage. Compared to the other models of the day, this one-ton engine, named Tom Thumb, looked almost like a toy.

Despite heckling, Cooper was sure his new machine would work. And work it did. On August 25, 1830, the machine chugged 7 miles (11 kilometers) in forty-five minutes.

But that wasn't all. For the return trip, a horse-driven railroad car challenged the new engine to a race. Peter Cooper accepted, fired up his engine, and headed down the tracks. Although the Tom Thumb was able to stay even with the horses for much of the way, it finally ran out of steam and was beaten. Even so, the little engine provided proof that the wave of the future was on the rails.

The Tom Thumb pulls past a horse-drawn car in a trial of speed.

As the trains themselves improved, more and more railroad companies sprang up around the country. There was the Erie Railroad of Pennsylvania. Cornelius Vanderbilt built the New York Central. A man named John Poor was responsible for a route from Portland, Maine, to Montreal, Canada; he surveyed every snowy inch of it himself.

It didn't take long for these lines to cover the eastern United States. But what about the West?

As early as 1832, a newspaperman in Ann Arbor, Michigan, wrote an editorial suggesting a cross-country railroad. At the time, when there were only 130 miles (209 kilometers) of track in the country, everyone thought him crazy.

This lithograph from the 1850s, "Westward the
Course of Empire Takes Its Way," expresses a typically
romantic vision of a continent linked by rail.

3

DRAWING THE ELEPHANT

America pushed west rapidly during the early 1800s. In 1803, Thomas Jefferson, the nation's third president, engineered the Louisiana Purchase, one of the great real estate steals of all time, in which France sold America much of the land west of the Mississippi. In 1805, Lewis and Clark reached Oregon Territory. Later, in the 1840s, Texas came into the Union, and Mormons settled Salt Lake City, Utah. Then the 1849 Gold Rush brought droves of settlers west to California.

As the country grew, convenient transportation lagged far behind. Ocean travel, around Cape Horn or to Central America, overland across the Isthmus, and up the Pacific coast, was possible. But the trip was long, costly, and dangerous. Most early settlers traveled by wagon train instead—a trip that took four to six months and often claimed many lives along the way.

In 1861, Ben Holladay established the Overland Stage line. But the trip took at least seventeen days at the steep price for those days of $225 per passenger. Not only that, a single trip across the country required the use of up to 2,700 fresh horses. And Indians, angered by this invasion of their lands, made safe arrival an uncertainty.

[17]

Feelings were mixed about the importance of building a transcontinental line. Many women and men agreed with Daniel Webster, one of the great U.S. senators of the day, who said, "What do we want of that vast and worthless area [the American West]?" Even if a railroad could be built across the country, what purpose would it serve?

But gradually the tide turned. As more and more people began to feel the lure of the West, they viewed a fast, affordable way of crossing the country as a necessity. The time of the cross-country railroad had come. The idea caught fire, and Congress was urged to act. Only one question remained: Which was the best route?

*B*UT HISTORICAL EVENTS were to conspire to delay the project. The late 1840s and 1850s were a time of great upheaval in America. The ugly issue of slavery was pushing the country toward civil war. Most Northerners thought slavery a moral wrong. Most Southerners, on the other hand, saw slavery as an economic necessity and felt it was their "states' right" to keep what was often called the "peculiar institution."

Amidst feelings this bitter, it was difficult, if not impossible, for Congress to concentrate on a transcontinental railroad—a project that many thought impossible or pointless in the first place. And when Congress did consider the problem, there was great debate over the route the railroad should take. After all, railroads meant trade, and trade meant money. Even in peaceful times, both the North and the South would have wanted the route to go through their territory.

The first option was presented to Congress in 1845. This route, the brainchild of the New York merchant Asa Whitney, was to begin in Chicago. Predictably, the Southern senators wouldn't have it. Then, in 1853, James Gadsden of South Carolina arranged for the government to buy a strip of desert land that stretched from the Rio Grande along the Mexican border to California. Not surprisingly, every Southern senator deemed what became known as the Gadsden Purchase as the shortest and cheapest way for a railroad west. But the Northerners vetoed the plan.

While Congress bickered, the life of the transcontinental was beginning out west. In 1859 a young engineer, Theodore Dehone Judah, arrived in California to help construct a 22-mile (35-kilometer) railroad between Sacramento and Folsom, California. Judah was probably the most committed of all transcontinental pioneers. The cross-country line was his consuming passion. "It will be built," he told his wife, "and I'm going to have something to do with it."

When the short, 22-mile railroad was completed, Judah set to work surveying the Sierra Nevada mountain range with an eye to a route east. That done, he did whatever he could to drum up interest in his idea. In fact, he was so persistent that he soon earned the nickname "Crazy Judah."

When all was said and done, Judah found four men to invest in his dream: Leland Stanford, future governor of California; Collis P. Huntington and Mark Hopkins, who had made their fortunes in hardware; and Charles Crocker, a dry-goods man. Known simply as the Big Four, these men approved Judah's plan and set up the Central Pacific Railroad. They told him, as a member of the board of directors, to go to Washington to petition the government for a loan.

By now, the Civil War had torn the nation in two; and all representatives and senators from the Southern states had left their seats in Congress to join the Confederacy. The now Northern Con-

Theodore Judah.
Facing page:
Officers of the
Central Pacific
Railroad.

gress saw that a railroad would help keep California and Nevada loyal to the Union cause at a time when the South appeared to be winning the war. And so, in 1862, Congress passed the Pacific Railroad Act: "An act to aid in the construction of a railroad and telegraph line from the Missouri River to the Pacific Coast, and to secure to the Government the use of the same for postal, military and other purposes."

OFFICERS of the CENTRAL PACIFIC RAIL ROAD

Specifically, the act called for the creation of the Union Pacific Railroad Company, which was to begin construction in Nebraska and build west until it met the Central Pacific, which would be starting in California and building east.

The two railroads were given "vacant" lands on each side of the track within 10 miles (16 kilometers). As further financial aid, the government would lend the two railroad companies bonds at the rate of $48,000 per mile for mountain construction, $16,000 per mile for track laid on the base of a mountain, and $32,000 for work done on the Sierra Nevada. These bonds would be payable in thirty years at 6 percent interest.

Obviously this act provided an enormous financial incentive to the builders. For every mile of track laid they were given ownership of 20 square miles (32 square kilometers) of land! But the lawmakers went even further. The act stated that if the Union Pacific should reach the California border before the Central Pacific, it might continue on, receiving government loan bonds and land rights for each extra mile. Similarly, if the Central Pacific arrived at the border first, it could forge forward, receiving the government benefits for each mile. This stipulation gave the heads of each railroad the perfect excuse to work their men to the bone to cover as much ground as possible.

In the midst of the Civil War, President Abraham Lincoln signed the Pacific Railroad Act into law. Theodore Judah returned to California a happy man. He had finally gotten the government backing necessary to work on his dream. But the building would not be easy. As Judah himself admitted in a wire to President Stanford of the Central Pacific: "We have drawn the elephant. Now let us see if we can harness him."

WORKIN' ON
THE RAILROAD

Ground-breaking ceremonies for the Central Pacific Railroad took place in Sacramento, California, on January 8, 1863.

On the chosen day it was pouring rain. The streets were mud baths. To great cheering from the assembled (and wet) crowd, Leland Stanford dug his spade into a tub of dirt someone had cleverly thought to cover up and keep dry for the ceremony.

"Everybody felt happy," the Sacramento *Union* said, "because after so many years of dreaming, scheming, talking and toiling, they saw with their own eyes the actual commencement of a Pacific railroad."

But even though they set to work with high spirits, the company found itself short of money almost immediately. Sale of Central Pacific bonds was very slow. Judah estimated that the first 50 miles (80 kilometers) of track would cost over $3 million, or $68,000 a mile. But the company had only $156,000 on hand, enough for slightly over 2 miles (3 kilometers). Even worse, the Central Pacific had to lay 40 miles (64 kilometers) of track before it would be eligible for government bonds and land grants. Huntington, one of the Big Four, went east looking for funds, but the Civil War made most investors extremely cautious.

So the Big Four, men not known for their honesty, did whatever they could to raise money. Stanford, now governor of California, was able to push through legislation in 1862 that authorized the state to issue bonds to be used for the purchase of Central Pacific stock. Then Stanford devised another scheme. The Central Pacific floated $12 million worth of bonds, but the interest on these bonds would be paid by the state, not the railroad.

With this newfound money, work proceeded. Even though these questionable business practices upset the honest Theodore Judah, he could do nothing legally to stop them: The building of his railroad had spun out of his control. He could only watch as the greedy Big Four did whatever it took to raise funds.

One of the Big Four's most ingenious and shady schemes was the brainchild of Huntington. The Pacific Railroad Act stated that it would pay out government loans of $48,000 a mile for track laid in the mountains, but only $16,000 for track on flatland. Huntington thought fast and got in touch with J. W. Whitney, the California state geologist, who told him that the base of the Sierra Nevada began where the brown earth of the Sacramento Valley met the red soil of the Sierras. Although scientifically this may have been true, the fact was that this stretch of land was totally flat. But President Lincoln, distracted by the war, approved the geologist's questionable interpretation, and the Central Pacific received $48,000 a mile for laying track over 24 miles (38 kilometers) of flat terrain! "Here is a case," said Charles Crocker, general superintendent of the railroad, "where Abraham's faith has moved mountains."

Judah was furious. True, he desperately wanted the railroad built, but not at the cost of dishonesty. Then came the final blow—

the Big Four offered to buy Judah out for $100,000. He accepted the offer but went by ship to New York anyway in the hope of raising enough funds to buy out the Big Four and place his "dream" railroad back under his own control. Sadly, Judah was bitten by a mosquito on his journey and contracted yellow fever. A week after he reached New York, he died, leaving the Central Pacific squarely in the hands of men he deemed unworthy to undertake such a noble enterprise.

$\mathcal{M}$EANWHILE, on the other side of the country, the Union Pacific was ladened with its own problems.

As with the Central Pacific, investors were scarce. At least the Central Pacific had the good fortune of having to lay only 50 miles (80 kilometers) of track before it could start earning profits transporting ore from mining towns. But the Union Pacific had to build a good 1,500 miles (2,400 kilometers) of track into the wilderness, through hostile Indian territory, before it could dream of making any sort of profit.

And there was debate over the proper starting point of the Union Pacific. Finally, in November 1863 (when the Central Pacific had been at work for almost two years), President Lincoln chose the city of Omaha, Nebraska.

Ground-breaking ceremonies for the Union Pacific Railroad were finally held on December 2, 1863. But shortage of funds delayed construction for another year and a half. The Union Pacific ran into the same problem that had plagued the Central Pacific—the railroad could not begin collecting government loans until it had laid at least 40 miles (64 kilometers) of track. But how could it lay this track—at a cost of at least $1 million—when it had no money?

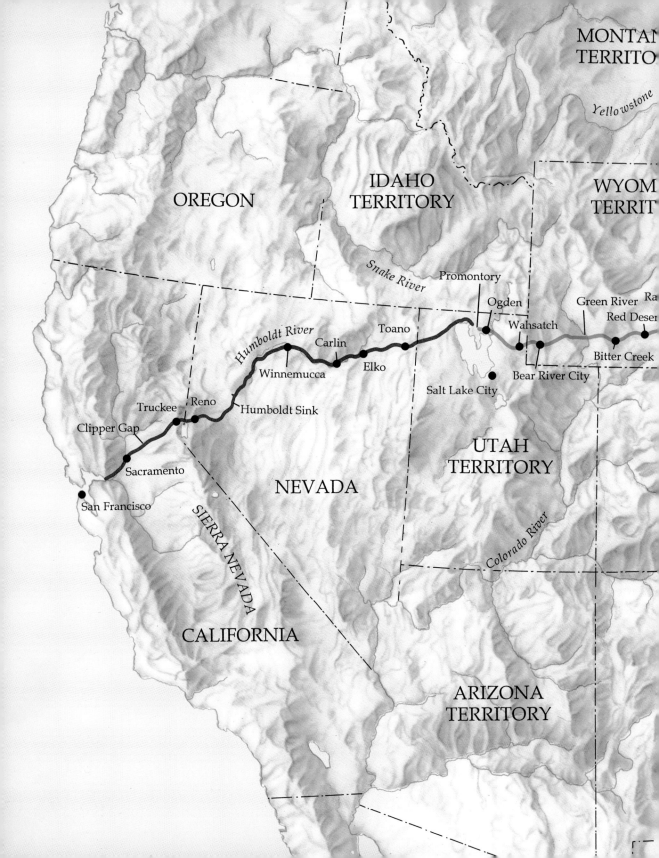

MONTAN[A]
TERRITO[RY]

Yellowstone

OREGON

IDAHO
TERRITORY

WYOM[ING]
TERRIT[ORY]

Snake River

Promontory

Ogden

Green River   Ra[wlins]
Red Deser[t]

Wahsatch

Bitter Creek

Humboldt River   Toano

Carlin

Winnemucca   Elko

Bear River City

Salt Lake City

Truckee   Reno

Humboldt Sink

Clipper Gap

UTAH
TERRITORY

Sacramento

San Francisco

NEVADA

S I E R R A   N E V A D A

Colorado River

CALIFORNIA

ARIZONA
TERRITORY

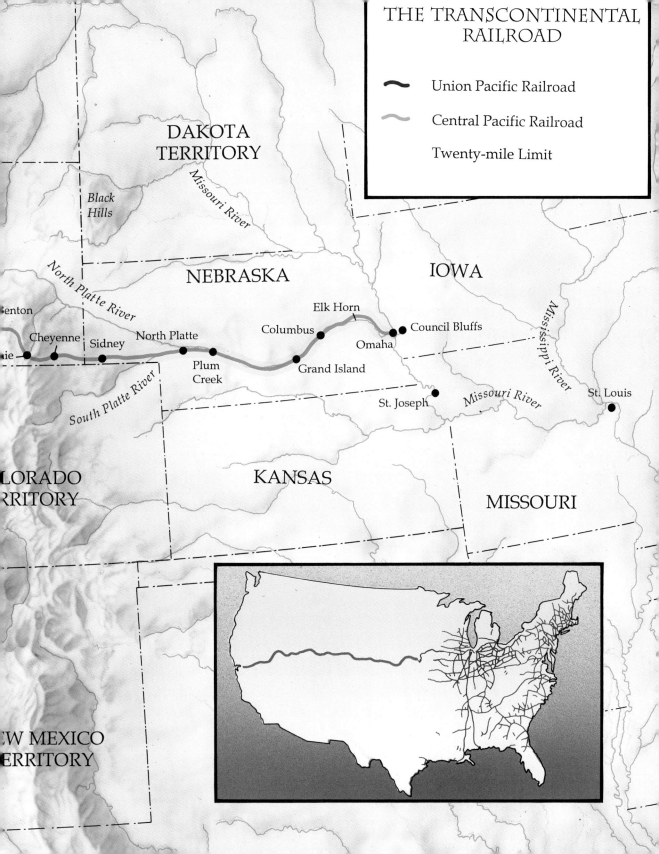

THE TRANSCONTINENTAL RAILROAD

~ Union Pacific Railroad

~ Central Pacific Railroad

Twenty-mile Limit

DAKOTA TERRITORY

Black Hills

Missouri River

NEBRASKA

North Platte River

IOWA

Mississippi River

Benton

Cheyenne

Sidney

North Platte

Plum Creek

Elk Horn

Columbus

Grand Island

Council Bluffs

Omaha

South Platte River

St. Joseph

Missouri River

St. Louis

COLORADO TERRITORY

KANSAS

MISSOURI

NEW MEXICO TERRITORY

President Lincoln came to the rescue the following July by signing the Pacific Railroad Act of 1864. This new law doubled the land grants the companies received for each mile of track laid. It also gave the companies mineral rights to this land. Finally, the act allowed the companies to sell their own bonds in amounts equal to the government bonds.

The leaders of both the Union and Central Pacific breathed a sigh of relief.

And now businessmen began to see dollar signs. Railroads were big business. To help raise even more money, Thomas Durant, chief investor in the Union Pacific, set up a company called Crédit Mobilier. This company contracted to build the railroad and then overcharged the government for its services. For example, Durant handed the contract for construction of the first 100 miles (160 kilometers) of the railroad over to a friend, Herbert M. Hoxie. Hoxie then billed the government $50,000 a mile for his services when the real cost was around $30,000. In this manner, Durant pocketed $20,000 for each mile built.

Chief engineer Peter Dey was outraged and promptly resigned. The post was soon filled by an ex-Union general, Grenville Dodge. Although Dodge was aware of Durant's shady business dealings, he couldn't resist being the chief engineer of such an exciting project. He did, however, warn Durant that he would accept the position only "on condition that I be given absolute control in the field. You are about to build a railroad through a country

Thomas Durant surveys the first miles of Union Pacific roadbed stretching west from Omaha, Nebraska.

that has neither law nor order, and whoever heads the work must be backed up. There must be no divided interests."

Despite this ultimatum, the two men would lock horns many times in the coming few years.

Both railroads sputtered forward then, the Union Pacific heading west through barren and often hostile territory, the Central Pacific doing its best to negotiate its tracks up the steep and treacherous Sierra Nevada mountains.

How could a group of workers, without the benefit of cranes, electric drills, or bulldozers, lay tracks across steep, snowy ranges? That was the challenge of the Central Pacific, a challenge they met through hard work and the unexpected arrival of some very special workers.

5

THE PUSH EAST

By June 1865, just as the Union Pacific was laying down its first rails, the Central Pacific had reached Clipper Gap, 43 miles (69 kilometers) from Sacramento. Here, at the edge of the Sierra Nevadas, the Big Four knew they would need a superior group of workers to face the daunting mountains. Sweeping cuts through rock would be required as well as costly detours to keep the track from becoming too steep for a train to climb. But many of the white laborers felt this dangerous work was worth far more than the $1 or $2 a day the railroad was willing to pay, especially when they could earn $4 a day working on the docks or maybe even strike it rich prospecting in the Nevada silver mines.

In fact, many of these men had no interest whatsoever in railroad work. They would sign on with the Central Pacific only for the free transportation to Clipper Gap. After working a week on the railroad, they would quit and head out to nearby mining towns to seek their fortune. (During one gold rush, two thousand workers were shipped to railroad camps and only one hundred of them stayed to work.)

Understandably, the Big Four were furious. They had to have a loyal, hardworking labor force. It was Charles Crocker who hit on a solution: Chinese immigrants.

Many people, however, thought this was a terrible idea. After all, most Chinese were tiny, often under 5 feet (152 centimeters) tall, weighing a mere 120 pounds (54 kilograms). How could people this small possibly be up to the physical demands of constructing a railroad over treacherous terrain? But Stanford, who had employed Chinese domestics in his home for years, backed Crocker up, and the Chinese came aboard.

The first group of Chinese to report—a group of fifty men wearing floppy blue cotton pants, basket hats, and blue blouses—were not made welcome by their fellow workers, the Irish in particular. Not only had the Irish borne the brunt of the country's heavy labor in the early 1800s, they had also been the object of much unfair ridicule. Now out west where he was finally accepted as a true American, the Irish worker was all too glad to dish out some of the abuse that had always been directed toward him.

Despite the whites' jeers, the Chinese impressed the Big Four. True, they couldn't dig as much dirt with a single swing of the shovel, but they worked methodically, without talking or taking breaks. Occasionally, they would stop for a quick cup of tea, but then get right back to their job. By the end of the first day of leveling terrain for tracks, they had covered as much distance as any all-white group and done the job more carefully.

Chinese crews in the High Sierra hacked shelves into the mountainside and then used axes and dynamite to even the grade before hauling the dirt and rocks away.

A late 1870s cartoon shows how anti-Chinese feelings were thinly disguised as patriotism.

CHINESE IMMIGRANTS

AMERICANS weren't the only people drawn to California by the 1849 gold rush. The thirst for overnight riches brought thousands of Chinese to the state. Though most of them did not strike it rich, they quickly established themselves as cooks, houseboys, gardeners, and laundrymen throughout the state. On the eve of the Civil War an estimated 42,000 of these "coolies" (the word *coolie* comes from a Hindu word meaning unskilled laborer) were at work in northern California. Although they were paid a low wage (usually a dollar a day), the Chinese were treated little better than slaves. They worked all day seven days a week and could be fired from any job on the spot for any reason. With well-earned reputations as hard workers, they seemed an ob-vious choice to work the Central Pacific.

By all rights, they should have been honored as California folk heroes for the fine job they did on the railroad. Chinese success bred even more racial tension. In San Francisco on March 6, 1867, a riot broke out; men and women roamed the streets throwing rocks and mud at Chinese establishments. That spring, hoodlums set fire to Chinese laundries and cigar factories. Some were known to howl obscenities at Confucian funeral processions.

This appalling behavior was largely based on the fear that the Chinese, having proved themselves a formidable work force, would take jobs from whites. A young journalist marveling at Chinese efficiency wrote: "What will happen when the Pacific Railroad is finished, and Chinese labor is loosed upon the rest of America?" Sadly, the harder the Chinese worked, the greater were the hostilities leveled against them.

Crocker was overjoyed. White laborers wanted $2 a day minimum, plus board. The Chinese agreed to work for $35 a month (slightly more than $1 a day) and a small amount of money for bamboo sprouts, sweet rice crackers, salted cabbage, and other Chinese foods, which they agreed to prepare themselves.

They may have been called "Crocker's pets," but by the fall of 1865, the Central Pacific had put three thousand of them to work. They proved talented in all aspects of construction.

With the Chinese help, the Central Pacific climbed slowly but surely to the top of the Sierra Nevada. There workers came upon the greatest obstacle of all—a giant cliff called Cape Horn. A roadbed had to be carved out of the cliff. Men would have to dangle by ropes while they hammered and drilled and blasted 2,500 feet (760 meters) above the American River.

The Chinese requested this job. To the sound of hooting whites, the Chinese wove baskets of reeds, in which workers were lowered down the face of the cliff. They drilled holes into the rock face and inserted gunpowder into them. After lighting the fuses, they were hauled back to the top before the explosion.

*B*Y MAY 1866, Cape Horn was clear and ready for track. And when the Grizzly Hill Tunnel was completed 10 miles (16 kilometers) to the east, even the Central Pacific's harshest critics had to agree that the railroad might well make it through the mountains and keep its date with the Union Pacific somewhere in Utah.

As chief engineer Charles Crocker goaded his workers on through that summer and fall, Central Pacific surveyors staked out a course down the Sierras to the Nevada border.

Then the harsh winter of 1866–1867 drove into Nevada bringing 10- to 20-foot-high (3- to 6-meter) snowdrifts. The men working on tunnels had to dig out 20 to 100 feet (6 to 60 meters) of snow before they reached the face of the cliff. Snowslides carried off many men—sometimes entire crews. The frozen bodies of many Chinese were found in the spring thaw, some with picks still lifted over their heads. Thousands of Chinese died during that dread winter, most from the cold, others after nitroglycerin blasts in the tunnels. It was in reference to these deaths that the phrase "not a Chinaman's chance" was coined.

As the Chinese died, Crocker and Stanford sent more to take their place. By the time the spring of 1867 finally came, the 12,000 Chinese at work in the Sierras had a right to feel proud of their efforts; they had braved horrible conditions to build a track over the top of the mountain, and they were now headed down the other side.

But on the way down another problem arose. Crocker and his chief engineer realized that the only way trains could be kept running during the winter was to build snowsheds—vast, peak-roofed tunnels that resembled covered bridges—over 37 miles (59 kilometers) of track. The Big Four sighed and, at a cost of $20,000 a mile, ordered them built. Some of the sheds had to be protected by gigantic stone walls to fend off snowslides and spring floods. Hundreds of Chinese masons worked during the winter of 1867–1868 completing these walls.

And so, through gargantuan efforts, the Central Pacific reached the California-Nevada border. But it didn't stop there. The rich farmland near Salt Lake City beckoned, promising steady profits for the first line to reach it. The Pacific Railroad Act stated that

Chinese workers cheer as a train enters a newly built snowshed in the Sierra Nevada range.

either railroad company could keep building and keep receiving government loans until it met the other. The Central Pacific, not about to pass up an opportunity like that, kept laying tracks as it waited for news from the Union Pacific.

6

"HELL ON WHEELS"

While the Central Pacific had to contend with the towering Sierra Nevada, the Union Pacific had the luxury of laying its first ties across flatland.

That did not mean that the work was easy. Oakes Ames, one of the directors of the Union Pacific, gave a concise summary of the hardships faced:

> *To undertake the construction of a railroad, at any price, for a distance of nearly seven hundred miles [1,126 km] in a desert and unexplored country, its line crossing three mountain ranges at the highest elevations yet attempted on this continent, extending through a country swarming with hostile Indians, by whom locating engineers and conductors of construction trains were repeatedly killed and scalped at their work; upon a route destitute of water, except as supplied by watertrains, hauled from one to one hundred and fifty miles [160–240 km], to thousands of men and animals engaged in construction; the immense mass of material, iron, ties, lumber, provision and supplies necessary to be transported from five hundred to fifteen hundred miles [800–2,400 km]. . . .*

To achieve such an awesome undertaking, an efficient way to haul supplies into the wilderness was a necessity. General Jack Casement and his brother Dan came to the rescue by inventing what came to be known as a Casement train, really an assembly line on wheels. The first car of this train was flat and held the rails needed to construct the track. Directly behind were other cars: a washhouse, sleepers, carpenters' shops, munitions storerooms—anything and everything that was useful was carted along.

And the workers had their tasks down to a science. Advance men walked before the Casement train, clearing way for the track. Behind them were the "joint-tie men" who methodically laid a railway tie every 14 feet (4 meters). After them, the "fillers" bedded the intervening ties. Then the strong "iron men" teamed up five to each rail—a rail weighing 700 pounds (317 kilograms)!—and lifted it onto the track. After the iron men came the "head spikers" who drove spikes into each rail. The "back spikers" and "screwers" finished spiking the rails and screwed on "fishplates," heavy iron clamps, on each side of the rail. Then "track liners" used crowbars to put the track in perfect line.

Complementing these workers directly engaged in the railroad's construction were others who loaded the iron rails shipped from the East onto the front flatcar and "water men" who made sure no one passed out in the heat. The list went on and on. Building a railroad was a finely tuned process.

*U*NFORTUNATELY, the route Dodge had mapped out through Kansas, across the Black Hills, took the Union Pacific track through the heartland of Sioux hunting grounds. Justifiably outraged by what they viewed as the trespassing white man, the Sioux were prepared

*General Jack Casement, dressed like a Cossack, poses
in front of the supply cars that bear his name.*

to fight for every inch of land. Moreover, the whites showed little respect for the territory they were invading. Buffalo were often killed for sport, whereas the Sioux held the land and its animals as sacred. When a Native American killed a buffalo, he made good use of every part of its body, from its meat to its hide.

Clashes were inevitable. Union Pacific workers, many of whom were Civil War veterans, became used to dropping their picks, runing to the munitions car, and grabbing a gun to ward off Indian attacks. These clashes became so frequent that in 1867 General Ulysses S. Grant (soon to be president) promised military protection to the tracklayers. But the end of the Civil War had led to great manpower cuts in the Army. Between Omaha and Denver there were only two hundred infantrymen. As one army officer observed: "It's hard to surround three Indians with one soldier."

The skirmishes continued. Sometimes Indians were driven to desperate measures to stop the railroad's forward march through their land. One group stretched a 40-foot-long (12-meter) leather rope across the track to block an oncoming train. This daring plan backfired when two Indians nearest the track were swept under the wheels. Other parties of Sioux and Cheyenne raced trains, shooting at the locomotives.

Then, on August 6, 1867, Chief Turkey Foot and his Cheyenne warriors successfully attacked and wrecked a train. In Plum Creek, 230 miles (370 kilometers) west of Omaha, the Indians ripped up rails and fastened ties to the track with telegraph wire. Five white men, led by William Thompson, were sent by handcar to check out the interruption of telegraph service. The handcar hit a ripped tie, turned a somersault, and flipped off the track. The men were chased down, and most of them were killed. Thompson himself survived but with a scalping. After the Indians were driven off

In Theodor Kaufmann's "Westward, The Star of Empire," Indians derail the tracks to keep the white man's iron horse from invading their land.

by white reinforcements, he traveled to Omaha with his scalp in a pail of water, where a doctor tried unsuccessfully to sew it back on his head.

But tragically for the Indians, these occasional victories could not impede the steady forward march of the railroad through their homeland.

$\mathcal{A}$ S THE TRACK moved deeper and deeper into the wilderness, towns called "hells on wheels" sprang up practically overnight to accommodate the laborers. Usually a single main street with a general store and a string of saloons, these towns flourished for short spurts then closed down as soon as the track pushed on. One traveler described the remnants of a deserted hell on wheels as nothing more than "a few posts and old chimneys, broken bottles and shattered oyster cans."

These towns usually attracted hard-living men and women who found temporary happiness over a shot of whiskey and a game of poker in a cheap saloon. The most infamous hell on wheels was Bear River City, near the Utah-Wyoming border, "the wickedest city in America." As one newspaperman, Henry M. Stanley, put it: "I verily believe there are men here who would murder a fellow creature for five dollars. . . . Not a day passes but a dead body is found somewhere in the vicinity with pockets rifled of their contents."

Another notorious hell on wheels was Cheyenne, Wyoming, located 517 miles (832 kilometers) west of Omaha. Here, crime got so out of hand that the mayor-magistrate, Luke Murrin, ordered that anyone caught firing a gun within city limits would pay a $10 fine. Even so, a "citizens' committee" had to hang at least twelve gunmen before the streets became somewhat safe.

And so the Union Pacific marched west, leaving a legacy of suffering, abandoned ghost towns, and wild stories in its wake.

This wild "hell on wheels" called Bear River
City sprang up with the railroad and disappeared
within a few months of its pushing through.

7

SHOWDOWN AT FORT SANDERS AND RACE TO THE FINISH

Years earlier, Grenville Dodge, chief engineer of the Union Pacific, had been sent to command a troop engaged in fighting the Native Americans in the West. During a scouting trip, Dodge and his cavalry were attacked. During their escape, Dodge discovered a pass through the Black Hills marked by a tree standing alone in the barren landscape.

Since that day, Dodge had felt that this so-called "lone-tree pass" would be the ideal spot for the Union Pacific to pass through the Black Hills.

But Thomas Durant, vice president of the Union Pacific, had other ideas. In late 1867 he ordered an alternate route through the Black Hills. Unfortunately, Durant's new route wasn't as good. Work stalled when his men got trapped in a December blizzard 8,000 feet (2,440 meters) up the mountains at Evans Pass. At this point the Union Pacific was 550 miles (885 kilometers) from Promontory, Utah, the spot where the two great tracks would eventually meet a year and a half later. (The Central Pacific was in Verde, Nevada, 557 miles—896 kilometers—from Promontory.)

To cover as much ground as possible, Dodge ordered work to begin before the spring thaw. He pushed his troops up the Black Hills, and when the weather grew warm, across the Red Desert.

Work proceeded steadily until Durant ordered yet another route change, claiming it would save money. But Dodge knew better. Durant's route was actually 20 miles (32 kilometers) longer. The only reason Durant suggested this new route was that he could receive government bonds for the extra miles of track laid. As Durant himself put it, his overriding goal had become to "grab a wad of money from the construction fees [on the railroad]—and get out."

General Dodge was furious. Luckily, General Grant, then the Republican nominee for president, was due in Laramie, Wyoming, in July for treaty talks with the Sioux. Also interested in the railroad, Grant wanted to inspect the tracks and ordered Durant and Dodge to meet him at Fort Sanders, in Laramie.

On July 26, 1868, the historic meeting took place. Grant, who had been asked to arbitrate the dispute between Durant and Dodge, told the two men to state their cases.

Durant charged that Dodge's route was "impossible" and had wasted money. When it was Dodge's turn, he explained why the changes Durant had ordered made no sense. He also pointed out it was unsound to run the line through Salt Lake City, home to the Mormons, just to satisfy their powerful leader, Brigham Young. "I cannot have financial interests dictating the layout of the line," Dodge said. "If change is insisted upon, I'll quit."

After a moment's consideration, Grant announced his verdict: "The Government expects this railroad to be finished. . . . And the Government expects General Dodge to remain with the road as its chief engineer until it is completed."

This group has just come from the historic showdown
between Grenville Dodge (far left) and Thomas Durant (slouched
on the fence behind top-hatted General Harney). General Grant
(in front of birdcage) sided with engineer Dodge.

And so the track pushed on, following Dodge's route, across the Red Desert where it climbed the plateau of the Continental Divide.

Then Dodge sought out chief engineer Samuel Montague of the Central Pacific. Dodge told Montague that the Union Pacific would be in Ogden, Utah, by the spring of 1869, and that in the interest of saving time and money the two railroads should decide upon a meeting place west of Ogden. Montague, who wanted to lay as much track as possible and reap the financial rewards for each mile, refused. Angry, Dodge returned to the Union Pacific, determined to work his men even harder.

*T*HE GREAT RACE between the U.P. and C.P. to outdo the mileage total of the other company was officially on.

And it didn't take long for the race to catch on with the press. As summer turned into fall, newspapermen rushed to the sites of both tracks, keeping the country up-to-date on the day-to-day progress of each line. The dispatches had the tenor of wartime correspondence: "Sherman with his victorious legions sweeping from Atlanta to Savannah was a spectacle less glorious than this army of men . . . binding across the broad breast of America the iron emblem of modern progress and civilization."

With all this hype and daily access to reports of the other railroad's progress, the U.P. and C.P. worked their men to the bone, setting new records for track laid per day. When word reached Jack Casement that the Chinese and Irish workers of the Central Pacific had slapped down 5 miles (8 kilometers) of track in one day, he ordered his men to do 6 miles (9 kilometers). Then in Granger, Wyoming, in late October, the Union Pacific men put down 7½ miles (12 kilometers). Upon receiving this news, Charles Crocker of the Central Pacific asserted: "The Central Pacific promises ten miles [16 kilometers] in one working day." Durant heard this news and saw yet another way to make some money. He wired Crocker: "Ten thousand dollars that you can't do it before witnesses." Crocker responded: "We'll notify you."

The railroads didn't make winter camp in 1869. Upset by news of Central Pacific progress, Durant ordered the U.P. workmen to keep on going through the harsh cold. Now the U.P. had to suffer as the C.P.'s Chinese had during the freezing winter in the Sierras. Timber had to be chopped out of snowbanks, track laid on ice.

Work under such conditions was ill-advised. When spring came, ice melted, leaving ties and rails dangling in midair. Sometimes the track would slide under the weight of the trains. Accidents and deaths increased, but Jack Casement and his foremen spurred the men on easily enough. Were the Union Pacific laborers going to let themselves be beaten by a bunch of Chinamen? Appealing to man's basest and most racist instincts, the Union Pacific was able to rally its troops and even find many men willing to work at night by lantern light in the freezing cold.

By late March of 1869, only 50 miles (80 kilometers) separated the two railroads. It was clear they would have to meet somewhere in the Promontory range, but neither side could agree where. In fact, both companies proceeded as though they were going to keep laying rail forever. Soon, Union and Central Pacific workers were digging parallel roadbeds only a few hundred feet from each other. (Before track was actually laid in the earth, a "roadbed" had to be dug to hold it.)

Someone with absolute authority had to take control. That someone was the new president, General Ulysses S. Grant. In

*By winter of 1868 the race was on. Advance U.P.
builders put up a temporary bridge over the Green River
(right) so the tracks could push through. Meanwhile,
they started to construct a bridge that would last (left).*

early April, Grant insisted that the two railroads pick a suitable spot to connect. Dodge, Durant, and Huntington of the Central Pacific worked out a pact: The C.P. would stop at Promontory if the U.P. would give them credit for government bonds for the track laid from Promontory east to Ogden.

And so it was agreed. But that still left one final piece of business. At the meeting, Crocker reminded Durant of their little bet: Ten thousand dollars said the C.P. workers couldn't lay 10 miles (16 kilometers) of track in a single day!

For the task, Crocker selected eight of his best Irish iron men (not Chinese, so as to avoid racial overtones). Then Crocker made sure everything was prepared. Railroad ties were distributed down the track. Carloads of rails and spikes were delivered at regular intervals.

Early that fateful day, these iron men—"sports heroes" of their day—got to work. They worked steadily and hard, stopping only for a quick sip of water. By one-thirty, they had laid 6 miles (9 kilometers) of rails. After lunch, Crocker offered to let any of the eight men quit. They all refused, and by seven that night they had laid 10 miles and 56 feet (17 kilometers) of track. During that busy day, 3,520 rails had been spiked. Each man had lifted an average of 250,000 pounds (113,400 kilograms) of iron.

Dodge was there to witness the awesome task. Though impressed, he did note that "they were a week in preparing for it, and bedded all their ties beforehand." But the U.P. men had no chance to prove themselves better, for after the record-breaking day, only 4 miles (6 kilometers) were left between the two tracks.

The next day, probably for the first time since the whole endeavor began, the workers laid track at a leisurely pace. On May 1, they stopped 58 feet (17.5 meters) apart. The Central Pa-

This sketch pokes fun at the competition between the Irish U.P. workers and the Chinese C.P. workers as the frenzied crews lay the last mile of track.

cific had gone 690 miles (1,110 kilometers) over the treacherous Sierra Nevadas. The Union Pacific had come 1,086 miles (1,747 kilometers) over mountains and Sioux hunting grounds.

The laborers lined up for their final paychecks and greeted their rivals face-to-face. As one newspaperman wrote, "The two opposing armies are melting away."

A U.P. poster advertises the comfort and excitement to be had along its transcontinental route, and the Chicago & Alton line promotes the luxury of Pullman cars that allow for sleeping and dining en route.

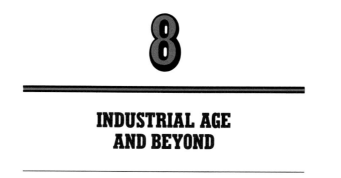

INDUSTRIAL AGE
AND BEYOND

Only a year after the two lines met, the Union Pacific attracted some unwanted attention when Congress discovered that the Crédit Mobilier Company had made up to a 200 percent profit on the construction of the railroad. Although the Union Pacific continued to run, it went bankrupt in 1893. But in 1897 a man named Edward H. Harriman reorganized the company, and the Union Pacific Railroad began to prosper.

While the Union Pacific ultimately kept its name and reputation, the Central Pacific lost its identity completely when it combined with the Southern Pacific in 1884. Today, Theodore Judah's dream railroad runs through the Sierra Nevadas under another name.

Despite changes in ownership and name, the transcontinental railroad brought great changes to the nation. In 1840 no towns and very few villages (aside from those of the Native Americans) populated that immense area of the country known as the American West. Fifty years later, twenty years after the railroad's completion, thousands of villages and over five thousand post offices had sprung up. With these new towns came newspapers, churches, schools, and universities.

Immigrants of many nationalities—Germans, Swedes, Norwegians, and others—made the move west. Most bought homesteads or worked on large farms and in towns. And the great trains helped these new settlers, carrying in farming machinery, then carrying produce to market. Farms flourished, and Kansas and Nebraska soon became known as the Breadbasket of America. Cattle and sheep farms sprang up all over the West, and cowboys led massive cattle drives from Texas and Mexico to Kansas, where the herds were shipped by rail to the rest of the country.

And once the transcontinental was working full force, other lines were built, fanning into the North and Southwest, giving those regions, too, the means to grow and prosper.

But the railroad had more than a purely economic use. The transcontinental opened up the country. "Every man who could command the time and money was eager to make the trip," wrote a travel reporter, John Beadle, "and everyone who could sling ink became correspondents."

The trip took eight to ten days, but most people didn't seem to mind. Stopovers in Chicago, Omaha, Promontory, or Ogden allowed people the luxury of getting to know their country.

And as service improved, travel by train became more exciting. People enjoyed the plush seats, the dining cars, and the "butcher boys" peddling candy and magazines.

But as these pleasure seekers rode the railroad into the frontier, most of them had little sense of the human sacrifice that was instrumental to its construction.

"The Great West,"
by Currier & Ives.

There were men such as "Crazy Judah," who surveyed the tough route over the Sierra Nevadas, then died before he could see his dream become a reality. There was Grenville Dodge, who fought every inch of the way against the terrain, the Indians, and even his own boss, to see the line completed in the best way possible. There were the laborers: the Chinese and Irish who sweated for up to ten years laying tie after tie under the worst of conditions for low wages. And tragically, there were the Native Americans who resisted without success the systematic destruction of their homelands.

But lurking behind any great accomplishment are great sacrifices and often a few tragedies. The fact remains that the construction of the transcontinental railroad remains one of the country's great early achievements. That strong band of iron bound the country firmly together and gave America the means to become a powerful industrialized nation.

Chronology

1804   British inventor Richard Trevithick first experiments with steam power.

1832   Newspaperman in Ann Arbor, Michigan, writes an editorial suggesting a transcontinental railroad.

1859   Theodore Judah builds railroad between Sacramento and Folsom, California, and surveys the Sierra Nevadas for a route east.

1860   Judah attracts the Big Four to invest in his dream, and the Central Pacific Railroad is founded.

1862   The Pacific Railroad Act is passed, providing government aid to the railroads and creating the Union Pacific Railroad.

1863   The Central Pacific begins work.

1864   The second Pacific Railroad Act is passed, providing more government aid. The Union Pacific finally has enough money to begin construction in Omaha, Nebraska.

1868   Famous meeting at Fort Sanders, in Laramie, Wyoming. General Ulysses S. Grant arbitrates a dispute between Grenville Dodge and Thomas Durant of the Union Pacific Railroad.

1869   The transcontinental railroad is completed in Promontory, Utah.

Further Reading

Harvey, T. *Railroads*. New York: Lerner Publications, 1980.

Jefferis, David. *Trains: The History of Railroads*. New York: Franklin Watts, 1991.

Kanetzke, Howard W. *Trains & Railroads*. Milwaukee: Raintree Publications, 1987.

MacDonald, Fiona. *A Nineteenth Century Railway Station: Inside Story*. New York: P. Bedrick Books, 1990.

Miller, Marilyn. *The Trans-Continental Railroad*. New York: Silver Burdett Press, 1985.

Stein, R. Conrad. *The Story of the Golden Spike*. Chicago: Childrens Press, 1978.

Bibliography

Ault, Phil. *"All Aboard."* New York: Dodd, Mead, 1976.

Brown, Dee. *Hear That Lonesome Whistle Blow.* New York: Holt, Rinehart and Winston, 1977.

Holbrook, Stewart H. *The Golden Age of Railroads.* Eau Claire, Wisc.: E. M. Hale, 1960.

Holland, Rupert Sargent. *Historic Railroads.* Philadelphia: MacRae, Smith, 1927.

Howard, Robert West. *The Great Iron Trail.* New York: G. P. Putnam's Sons, 1962.

Johnson, Enid. *Rails Across the Continent.* New York: Julian Messner, 1965.

Latham, Frank B. *The Transcontinental Railroad 1862–69.* New York: Franklin Watts, 1973.

McCready, Albert. *Railroads in the Days of Steam.* New York: American Heritage, 1960.

Index